REAL ESTATE
BUSINESS
FUNDAMENTALS

*THE 7 HIGH STRESS, NEGATIVE CASH FLOW
MISTAKES TO AVOIDE SO THAT YOU CAN:*

- *BUILD GENERATIONAL WEALTH*
- *HAVE CONFIDENCE*
- *SYSTEMATIZE YOUR BUSINESS*

*"Without awareness, growth is merely a façade, for true success lies in
uncovering and overcoming the hidden barriers." - Shawn Tiberio*

SHAWN TIBERIO

Address all inquiries to:
Shawn Tiberio
Telephone: 818-717-7577
Email: Shawn@REIToolBox.com
www.REIToolBox.com
www.ShawnTiberio.com
ISBN: 9798861445054

Every attempt has been made to properly source all quotes.
Printed in the United States of America

First Edition
2 4 6 8 10 12

Introduction

This book is not about how to get rich quick in real estate. It's about how to build a sustainable, profitable business that will generate generational wealth for you and your family. But first, you need to avoid the seven silent killers that can derail your business before it even gets started.

The Seven Silent Killers

1. Not having a clear vision. What do you want your business to look like in five years? Ten years? Once you know what you want, you can start to develop a plan to get there.
2. Not understanding your market. Who is your ideal customer? What are their needs and wants? Once you understand your market, you can tailor your marketing and sales efforts accordingly.
3. Not having a system for generating leads. Where are you going to find motivated sellers? How are you going to contact them? Once you have a system in place, you'll be able to generate leads on a consistent basis.
4. Not having a proven sales process. What do you say to potential sellers? How do you handle objections? Once you have a proven sales process, you'll be able to close more deals.
5. Not having a team in place. You can't do everything yourself. You need to build a team of experienced professionals who can help you with all aspects of your business, from marketing to closing deals.

6. Not investing in your business. You need to invest in marketing, training, and technology in order to stay ahead of the competition.
7. Not being patient. Building a successful real estate business takes time and effort. Don't expect to get rich quick.

How to Avoid the Seven Silent Killers

Now that you know what the seven silent killers are, here's how to avoid them:

1. Have a clear vision. Take some time to think about what you want your business to look like in five years, ten years, and beyond. Once you know what you want, write it down and create a plan to get there.
2. Understand your market. Who is your ideal customer? What are their needs and wants? Do some research to learn as much as you can about your target market.
3. Have a system for generating leads. There are many different ways to generate leads, such as networking, online marketing, and direct mail. Find a system that works for you and stick to it.
4. Have a proven sales process. What do you say to potential sellers? How do you handle objections? Practice your sales pitch and be prepared to answer any questions that sellers may have.
5. Build a team. You can't do everything yourself. Identify the key skills and experience that you need in your business and start building a team to support you.
6. Invest in your business. Set aside a budget for marketing, training, and technology. Investing in your business will help you to grow and succeed.
7. Be patient. Building a successful real estate business takes time and effort. Don't expect to get rich quick. Stay focused on your vision and keep working hard, and you will eventually achieve your goals.

The real estate business can be very rewarding, but it's important to avoid the seven silent killers that can derail your business before it even gets started. By following the tips in this book, you can avoid these pitfalls and build a successful real estate business that will generate generational wealth for you and your family.

As a seasoned real estate investor, national trainer, and marketing visionary, I've seen firsthand the devastating impact of the seven silent killers. That's why I wrote this book: to share my insights and help you avoid these common pitfalls.

By following the advice in this book, you can build a sustainable, profitable real estate business that will generate generational wealth for you and your family.

About the Author

Shawn Tiberio is a distinguished figure in the realm of real estate investment, with an impressive portfolio spanning over a decade of successful deals and ventures. As a seasoned real estate investor, he has masterfully executed hundreds of transactions, amassing a wealth of experience that sets him apart as a true industry expert.

Recognized on a national scale, Shawn Tiberio has earned a reputation not only as an accomplished investor but also as a revered real estate trainer and marketing luminary. His insights into the intricate interplay between real estate and marketing have positioned him as a trailblazer, guiding both budding and seasoned professionals through the intricacies of the field.

With a passion for sharing knowledge, Shawn Tiberio authored the acclaimed book "Marketing is Like Dating: The Ultimate Guide to Marketing for Real Estate Experts." This literary endeavor serves as a testament to his dedication to educating and empowering others in the real estate domain.

Adding to his repertoire of accomplishments, Shawn Tiberio is the host of the WebBuzz podcast, where he engages with industry leaders and dives deep into discussions that fuel the growth and evolution of real estate practices.

At the helm of REIToolbox, a pioneering force in real estate marketing, Shawn Tiberio assumes the role of CEO, spearheading innovation and redefining marketing strategies for the industry.

His leadership has solidified REIToolbox's position as an industry leader and a go-to resource for real estate professionals seeking to elevate their marketing endeavours.

Shawn Tiberio's multifaceted journey is a testament to his unwavering commitment to propelling the real estate landscape forward. Through his expertise, leadership, and dedication to continuous improvement, he continues to shape the industry's trajectory, leaving an indelible mark on real estate, training, and marketing.

Table of Contents

In this chapter, we'll delve into the first silent killer: intense competition. The real estate market is dynamic, and the number of investors seeking motivated seller leads has grown significantly. We'll explore how to stand out amidst the competition, differentiate your business, and target the right sellers effectively.

The second silent killer is flawed marketing strategies. It's essential to assess your marketing efforts to ensure they resonate with your target audience. We'll discuss the importance of identifying your ideal sellers, refining your marketing tactics, and leveraging digital tools to attract motivated leads.

Chapter three examines the influence of market conditions and trends on finding motivated sellers. We'll navigate through seller's markets, buyer's markets, and transitional periods, helping you adapt your approach to prevailing conditions and optimize lead generation efforts.

In this chapter, we'll address the power of networking and relationship-building in real estate. Establishing meaningful connections with potentially motivated sellers can unlock off-market opportunities. Learn how to build trust, nurture connections, and expand your network to gain access to exclusive deals.

Chapter Five highlights the significance of thorough research in your real estate journey. Understanding local market trends, identifying potential motivated sellers, and assessing their needs will position you for success. We'll explore various research techniques to refine your lead-generation process.

The sixth silent killer deals with ineffective lead-generation techniques. Discover innovative and proven strategies for generating high-quality leads. From direct mail campaigns to digital marketing, we'll explore various channels to increase your chances of attracting motivated sellers.

In the final chapter, we explore the importance of effective communication when dealing with motivated sellers. Clear and compelling communication builds trust and confidence, making sellers more inclined to consider your offers. Learn how to communicate with empathy, negotiate effectively, and close deals successfully.

By completing "The 7 Silent Killers Keeping Your Real Estate Business from Growing." Armed with this knowledge, you will be better equipped to overcome the obstacles hindering your growth as a real estate investor. Remember, success in real estate hinges on continuous learning, adaptability, and perseverance. By implementing the strategies outlined in this book, you can navigate the challenges, unlock new opportunities, and achieve sustainable growth in your real estate business.

CHAPTER 1

Intense Competition

"In the midst of chaos, there is also opportunity." - Sun Tzu

Blazing Your Own Trail in a Competitive Real Estate Market

Operating in the highly competitive world of real estate investing comes with intense pressures that can be difficult to navigate. With so many rival investors vying for the same limited pool of motivated seller leads, it's easy to fall into the trap of conformity and simply follow the herd. However, taking the well-trodden path and mimicking the tactics of others will only lead to mediocrity. To truly thrive amidst fierce competition, you must break free from convention and forge your own unique path to success.

The Perils of Conformity

The temptation to conform is omnipresent in crowded markets teeming with competitors. Adhering to established industry norms and mirroring your rivals' strategies may seem like a rational choice for survival. But in the long run, conformity chokes creativity and innovation - the true drivers of sustainable competitive advantage and exponential business growth.

By fixating on what appears to be currently working for others, you restrict your field of vision, overlooking nascent opportunities. Your business strategies become derivative, devoid of the ingenuity required to capture attention and mindshare in an increasingly noisy marketplace. Conformity breeds complacency, causing your skills and offerings to stagnate while hungrier competitors sprint ahead with disruptive new approaches tailored to shifting market demands.

Over time, conformity strips away the distinctive attributes that set your real estate business apart. By bluntly following the herd, you fade into the background, becoming just another forgettable face among the masses. This lack of differentiation diminishes your visibility and weakens your value proposition. Without a compelling reason for motivated sellers to choose you over alternatives, attracting high-quality leads and conversions becomes an uphill battle.

In the intensely competitive real estate arena, businesses that take the path of least resistance get left behind. Settling for safety and predictability instead of embracing risk and ingenuity is a slow slide into obscurity. To thrive amid cutthroat competition, you must rebel against conformity's stranglehold and unlock your enterprise's latent innovative potential.

Claim Your Competitive Edge

To break free from the perils of conformity, start by looking inward and identifying your organization's unique strengths and capabilities. What resources, knowledge, or expertise do you possess that competitors lack? Dig deep to uncover your special sauce - those distinctive qualities intrinsic to your real estate business.

Perhaps your competitive advantage lies in proprietary data, bespoke technology solutions, or exclusive partnerships. You may boast unrivaled experience serving a specific geography, property type, or client niche. Or your edge could stem from an exceptional company culture that attracts top talent. Your founding principles and purpose may differentiate you from transaction-focused rivals. Identify exactly where your enterprise shines brightest to pinpoint areas ripe for differentiation.

The next step is prominently spotlighting your rare qualities across all brand messaging and client touchpoints. Consistently showcase your specialized market mastery, client service excellence, or ability to deliver added value. Make your competitive differentiation impossible for motivated sellers to ignore. Craft compelling narratives that highlight why your solutions uniquely address their pain points compared to alternatives.

Back up your claims of distinctiveness with concrete proof points. Quantify your advantage through metrics demonstrating higher satisfaction scores, shorter sale times, bigger cost savings, or other tangible benefits driven by your competitive edge. The more persuasive evidence you provide to validate your uniqueness, the easier it is for leads to recognize and gravitate toward your differentiated value proposition.

Achieving differentiation requires more than just talk. You must deliver tangibly on the promise of your competitive advantage through superior service levels, product innovation, and optimization of processes to maximize efficiency. Maintaining your hard-won edge takes constant vigilance and improvement to stay ahead as rivals react and the industry evolves. But doubling down on your points of distinction gives motivated sellers compelling incentives to partner with you over competitors.

Cultivate a Culture of Innovation

Conformity is often the path of least resistance. But settling for business as usual is a recipe for stagnation in hyper-competitive real estate markets. To sustain differentiation and become an industry innovator, you must actively nurture a culture celebrating creative thinking and change.

Empower your team to challenge orthodoxies and established practices. Make brainstorming alternative solutions and strategies a regular activity. Questioning the status quo prepares your mindset to recognize untapped opportunities and pioneer inventive new approaches competitors will scramble to emulate.

Make continuous skills development a priority across your organization. Send promising employees to specialized training programs to expand expertise in key competitive arenas like data analytics or digital marketing. Bring in experts for knowledge sharing workshops on bleeding-edge industry trends. Upskilling and fresh perspectives break you out of habitual thought patterns vulnerable to conformity.

Establish innovation goals and key performance indicators to incentivize the kinds of behaviors that spark ingenuity. Recognize and reward employees who disrupt the old ways of doing things or deliver impressive results from implementing original ideas. Foster healthy inter-team collaboration and information flows to cross-pollinate thinking. Make innovation intrinsic to your culture.

Of course, not every new idea pans out. Failure is part of the innovation game. Establish mechanisms like proof-of-concept testing to quickly validate promising concepts and cull less viable ones before over-committing resources. As long as you keep learning and improving, failed experiments are not wasted effort, but rather stepping stones toward breakthroughs. The rewards of a true innovation culture make occasional misses well worth the risks.

Claim Your Rightful Place as an Industry Leader

In competitive real estate markets, mediocrity and conformity lead to being swallowed up by the crowd. But by purposefully leveraging your rare strengths and innovating beyond the status quo, you distinguish your business, delight motivated sellers, and spur exponential growth.

Stay laser-focused on delivering client outcomes predicated on your competitive advantage. Consistently refine strategies to widen your differentiation gap from pursuing rivals. Build a reputation for upending stagnant industry practices and norms. Be recognized as a visionary pioneer blazing new trails to the future.

It takes courage and grit to resist conformity's gravitational pull when others seem content riding established waves of success. But mindless imitation breeds forgettable sameness, while purposeful differentiation builds iconic brands.

The competitive arena only has room for a few real trailblazers and market leaders. Will you be among them? The choice is yours: conform to conventions of the past and become obsolete, or break molds and innovate to claim market leadership today and enduring industry dominance tomorrow. The future belongs to the bold. Blaze your own trail and motivated sellers seeking a superior real estate experience will eagerly follow your path.

Conclusion

In the dynamic real estate arena, intense competition is a relentless fact of life. Yet within this daunting challenge lies the opportunity to transform your enterprise from just another face in the crowd into an industry titan leading markets of the future. Seizing this opportunity requires an unwavering commitment to continuous innovation in everything you do.

The first step is liberating your organization from the shackles of conformity. Conventional wisdom only delivers conventional results. To unleash exponential growth, you must diverge boldly from the beaten path. Have the courage to question stale industry orthodoxies and pioneer new strategies aligned to evolving market needs.

By embracing your company's unique identity and capabilities, you crystallize a compelling value proposition that resonates amid the competitive noise. Broadcast your differentiators loudly and consistently across every brand touchpoint and client interaction. Make your distinctiveness impossible for motivated sellers to ignore.

Leverage emerging technologies to engage audiences on deeper levels and gain data-driven insights into their motivations. Let analytics guide your marketing with surgical precision. Turn each digital touchpoint into a bespoke experience that fosters lasting connections beyond transactions.

While leaning on data, don't lose sight of the power of empathy and outstanding customer service. Treat every motivated seller with respect and professionalism. Make their challenges your own, and craft solutions that ease their pain points better than any competitor. Earn trust and loyalty through exceptional experiences.

Remember that innovation is not a one-time project but an endless pursuit. The competition never sleeps, so you must constantly improve and refine your value proposition to stay ahead. Nurture a culture of creativity that challenges the status quo and embraces smart risks. Make innovation intrinsic to your DNA.

The road is long, with many twists and turns. You will face setbacks amidst successes. But commitment to continuous progress unlocks dormant potential within your people, processes and strategies. Over time, the compounding advantages of innovation establish your enterprise as an industry trailblazer that competitors struggle to match.

The arena of real estate competition will only intensify as technology and markets evolve. Settlement for satisfactory progress hands victory to hungrier players. But by forging your own path, unlocking innovation at scale and delivering unmatched value to motivated sellers, you secure a seat among the elite industry leaders of today and iconic brands of tomorrow.

The future belongs not to the conformists clinging to past formulas, but to the innovators and pioneers unafraid to reinvent the game. With relentless innovation as your compass, growth, prosperity and competitive dominance will follow for your real estate business. The time for you to seize the future is now. Step forward boldly.

CHAPTER 2

Flawed Marketing Strategies

*"Good marketing makes the company look smart.
Great marketing makes the customer feel smart." - Joe Chernov*

Crafting a Magnetizing Real Estate Marketing Strategy

In the dynamic realm of real estate investing, a stellar marketing strategy is the compass that guides you through the intricacies of attracting and connecting with motivated sellers. Far from a one-and-done checklist item, marketing requires an unwavering commitment to understanding your audience, optimizing your presence across channels, testing new approaches, and continuously improving based on hard data.

Constructing a marketing strategy that truly resonates requires laying a foundation of intimate audience understanding. You must dig deep beyond basic demographics to uncover the hopes, dreams, and fears of your ideal motivated sellers.

Fostering Deep Audience Intimacy

Truly stepping into the shoes of your potential clients is a multifaceted endeavor that requires dedicating time to research, surveys, interviews, and analysis. Learn everything you can about the pain points that keep your audience up at night when it comes to their real estate needs. What problems are they grappling with? What outcomes are they seeking? What fears or uncertainties might be holding them back?

These frustrations likely differ across audience segments. Retirees looking to downsize may fear losing their community connections, while growing families struggle with lack of space. Listen closely to understand each group's unique situation.

Move beyond facts and data by getting to know your audience's mindsets. What words and ideas resonate most with their worldview? How do they perceive the home selling process? Where do they look for solutions? Immersing yourself in their paradigm allows you to communicate in a way that powerfully connects.

Weave everything you learn into detailed buyer personas. Give each target audience segment a name and backstory so they become living, breathing people in your mind. Refer back regularly to keep their hopes and challenges front and center as you craft content and campaigns.

This deep audience intimacy informs every facet of your marketing. When you know their hearts and minds, you can create messaging that feels like it was crafted just for them. Your content will address the questions they have and provide the solutions they seek.

Optimizing Your Real Estate Website

Your website is the 24/7 digital embodiment of your real estate business. A magnetizing online hub draws in motivated sellers and builds credibility through top-notch user experience.

- **Design for trust.** A clean, modern website with engaging yet professional visuals signals you are an authoritative industry resource clients can rely on.

- **Simplify navigation.** Make it effortless for visitors to find what they need. Include logical site menus, a prominent property search tool, and clear calls-to-action across every page.

- **Share know-how**. User-friendly site content like FAQs, market reports, neighborhood guides and step-by-step explanations shows you're committed to education and transparency.

- **Spotlight social proof**. Sprinkle in testimonials, ratings and reviews to provide reassurance you deliver results.

- **Offer lead magnets**. Free tools like savings calculators entice visitors to share contact info so you can continue nurturing them as leads.

- **Mobile optimization is mandatory.** Ensure site speed, navigation, forms and other elements work flawlessly on smartphones so you never miss connecting with potential sellers on the go.

- **Monitor analytics**. Site traffic, bounce rates, time on page and other metrics provide guidance for continuously improving performance.

Cultivating Connections on Social

In 2023, having an engaging social media presence is no longer optional for real estate professionals seeking to thrive. Platforms like Facebook and Instagram allow you to build genuine connections by sharing your passion, expertise and insights.

- **Educate and entertain**. Share market trends, selling tips, behind-the-scenes peeks, and more. Provide value beyond promoting yourself.

- **Get visual.** Photos, infographics, and videos breathe life into your expertise. Avoid text-heavy posts.

- **Tell success stories**. With their permission, spotlight clients you've helped. This social proof builds trust.

- **Converse; don't broadcast**. Reply to every comment. Answer questions thoughtfully. Building relationships takes ongoing dialogue.

- **Run contests and quizzes**. Fun content formats foster engagement. Fans love sharing their results.

- **Stay responsive**. Reply promptly to inquiries. Don't make followers wait for your assistance.

- **Optimize hashtags**. Include relevant ones that help people find your posts. #realestate and #realtor are good starters.

- **Cross-promote content**. Share website blog posts on social networks to maximize reach.

- **Analyze performance**. Track engagement and follower growth. Lean into what resonates most with your audience.

Captivating Through Email Marketing

Email is one of the most direct ways to nurture relationships with potential motivated sellers over time. Avoid an impersonal spray-and-pray approach by crafting emails as valuable touchpoints.

- **Segment and personalize**. Group your list by factors like location or property type. Customize emails accordingly.

- **Surprise and delight**. Send unexpected value like market reports, neighborhood guides and savings hacks.

- **Share insider tips**. Offer exclusive advice tailored to each segment's needs to show you're paying attention.

- **Nurture with drip campaigns**. For example, provide first-time sellers with a pre-written series of helpful tips over weeks or months.

- **Tell stories**. Share case studies detailing how you helped other clients navigate challenges.

- **Make it mobile-friendly**. With over half of emails opened on smartphones, mobile optimization is a must.

- **Test subject lines**. Try different options and see which get the most opens. Adjust based on performance.

- **Time it right**. Pay attention to when your audience is most likely to open. Early morning or midweek evenings tend to see higher open rates.

- **Monitor analytics**. Open rates, clickthroughs, etc. point the way toward creating even better emails going forward.

Running Targeted Paid Ads

While organic marketing builds critical foundation, paid advertising turns up the volume on your message. With careful targeting, compelling creative and testing, paid platforms like Google and Facebook help you connect with your ideal prospects.

- **Define your audience**. Use what you know about your ideal buyer demographics, interests and behaviors to narrow your focus.

- **Zone in on location**. Target ads regionally or locally to attract sellers in specific areas.

- **Test design variations**. Try different ad copy, headlines, images and calls-to-action to see what resonates.

- **Drive traffic to strong lead magnets** like quizzes, savings calculators and neighborhood guides that incentivize contact info sharing.

- **Retarget engaged visitors** with additional promotions to keep your brand top of mind.

- **Track conversions** from calls, form fills and other actions, not vanity metrics like clicks or impressions.

- **Optimize campaigns continuously**. Use performance data to double down on what works and improve what doesn't.

- **Coordinate with larger strategy**. Integrate digital ads with direct mail, events and other initiatives for omni-channel impact.

While paid ads require financial investment, the potential returns from connecting with more of your ideal buyers make them well worth incorporating into your marketing mix.

Relentless Improvement Through Testing and Analysis

In the fast-changing digital landscape, real estate marketing is no place for complacency. The most effective marketers adopt a growth mindset founded on continuous testing, learning and optimization.

- **Experiment with new platforms** like TikTok or pod-casting to evaluate emerging avenues to reach buyers. Be willing to fail fast and course correct.

- **A/B test ad creatives** like different headlines or call-to-action language to see what resonates most.

- **Personalize** based on user behaviors like frequently searched locations or properties recently viewed.

- **Embrace attribution modeling** to quantify how each marketing channel contributes to conversions.

- **Refine spending** accordingly.

- **Interview past clients** to identify areas where you could improve messaging or content quality to build even stronger connections.

- **Monitor the latest real estate marketing innovations** like digital closing tools or 3D home tours and evaluate whether they could enhance your business.

- **Set goals and benchmarks** for lead quantity, cost per conversion, website traffic increases and other KPIs to systematically measure progress.

While an obsessive focus on audience experience, not vanity metrics, should drive marketing, having concrete goals creates accountability to execute on ongoing improvement.

Real estate marketing is never "set and forget." To attract the maximum number of ideal motivated sellers, you must continually optimize based on in-depth audience understanding, campaign data, customer feedback and an innovative mindset. Agile marketers who embrace constant learning and evolution will thrive amid endless change.

The rewards of dedicating yourself to mastering marketing are immense. Thoughtful messaging and experiences which speak to the core of your audience build credibility and emotional bonds beyond what competitors can match. When potential sellers feel deeply understood, they will entrust you with one of their most valuable assets - the sale of their home. By following the principles of audience-centric, data-driven marketing, you are laying the foundation for an abundantly prosperous real estate business for years to come.

CHAPTER 3

Market Conditions and Trends

"In the business world, the rearview mirror is always clearer than the windshield." - Warren Buffett

Mastering Motivated Sellers Across Market Cycles

The availability of motivated sellers fluctuates dramatically based on real estate market conditions. When supply is low and demand is high in a sellers' market, finding homeowners willing to sell at favorable prices becomes intensely competitive. Meanwhile, abundant choices coupled with fewer buyers in a buyers' market create different yet equally important challenges. Savvy investors must continuously adapt their strategies and messaging to capitalize on opportunities across market cycles. Developing this adaptability takes dedication to understanding data, expanding networks and creativity.

Cultivating Success in a Sellers' Market

Sellers' markets, where demand for properties exceeds supply, require digging deeper to find hidden gems. With homeowners less financially motivated to sell, unconventional channels and approaches become essential.

Network extensively to find off-market deals before they list. Attend local real estate investor meetings to connect with like-minded professionals who can be sources of deals. Build rapport with homeowners by being involved in community organizations and events. Survey everyone in your network for leads—friends, family, colleagues, vendors you work with. Many future deals start from these trusted relationships.

Mine niche opportunities overlooked by less specialized investors. Markets with military bases, universities or major employers see frequent turnover. Executor sales after inheritance present win-win scenarios. Out-of-state owners of investment properties might be persuaded to sell below-market when tired of managing long distance.

Get creative with deal structures and terms to provide incentives when inventory is scarce. Offer homeowners future equity participation, split proceeds or seller financing. Add lease-to-own provisions giving tenants purchase rights. Be flexible to close unconventional deals.

Position yourself as a motivated seller's best solution. Showcase your ability to address uncertainties and make the process smooth. Provide comparisons to recent area sales so sellers understand their options. Share success stories of facilitating profitable, quick closings for happy clients. Build a reputation for getting motivated sellers to the finish line.

Amid limited choice, your sharpened expertise, strong relationships and creative problem solving make you the investor sellers seek when ready to move.

Opportunities in Buyers' Markets

In buyers' markets with plentiful properties and lagging demand, motivated sellers may struggle to sell quickly or at desired prices. This shift opens doors for investors who provide solutions.

Identify diamonds in the rough with untapped potential. Driven sellers may list below-market to attract buyers. Sort through abundant options to spot fixers with strong bones in desirable areas. Look for cosmetic issues masking underlying quality. Patiently acquire underpriced properties and add value through renovations.

Structure creative win-win agreements tailored to motivated sellers' needs. Offer quick cash closings to provide urgently required liquidity. If reluctant to sell below purchase price, include future equity sharing provisions when you sell for profit. Installment sales help sellers defer capital gains tax. Lease-to-own arrangements keep displaced sellers housed while finding new permanent homes.

Cast yourself as a lifeline for stressed sellers. Many feel lost navigating extended sale timelines and negotiations. Provide expert guidance on pricing, staging and listing strategies. Share your network of agents, contractors and other professionals to streamline the process. Be a trusted advisor at every step.

Project reassurance amid ambiguity. Market downturns understandably worry and confuse sellers. Educate them on historical cycles using concrete examples of how markets eventually rebound. Demonstrate how selling now can be prudent depending on personal situations. Your consultative approach builds trust in turbulent times.

Patience, creativity and win-win problem solving position you to profit when competitors only see daunting challenges in saturated buyers' markets. Motivated sellers will flock to you for solutions.

Nimble Navigation Through Transitional Periods

The winds of real estate markets constantly shift based on economic trends, interest rates, regulations and other macro factors. The interludes when markets flip from buyers' to sellers' present a complex maze of uncertainty. Nimble investors who quickly adapt strategies reap substantial rewards in changing conditions.

Closely monitor data and news to recognize impending transitions before the general public. Follow mortgage rates, housing starts data, and consumer sentiment surveys. Watch for new government policies on development incentives, lending rules or homeowner subsidies that could tilt conditions. Accurately anticipating turns lets you pivot faster than competitors.

Build flexibility into business operations to take advantage of fluctuating circumstances. Lighter overhead and variable contractor costs allow you to ramp up/down volume to match opportunity. Maintain access to financing so you can act quickly when deals surface. Option rather than outright buy land/ properties when the future is unclear.

Forge networks as a stabilizing force when markets are in flux. Develop a broad spectrum of relationships - investors, agents, contractors, hard money lenders, etc. Bounce ideas off your experienced team when the playbook keeps changing. Lean on your advisors to navigate uncertainty.

Remain agile with deal structures. Be willing to try creative new purchase terms that address sellers' evolving needs in changing dynamics. Add working capital loans and delayed settlements. Swap land for equity. Bridge the gap with short-term owner financing. Adaptability opens more doors.

Real estate's constantly moving parts require resilience and willingness to evolve. By embracing analytics, flexibility and creativity, transitional times become your opportunity to shine while competitors flounder. You build a reputation as a guide through uncertain waters. When markets shift, motivated sellers will turn to your expertise and solutions to chart the best course ahead.

Impacts of Technology and Disruption

Real estate's trajectory has been irreversibly altered by technology. From analytics unlocking insights to platforms enabling seamless transactions, investors must continuously adapt to evolving digital tools and models or risk obsolescence. Progress marches on steadily, but humble students of change prosper.

Expand your virtual presence to engage motivated sellers where they spend time. Share market perspectives and success stories on social media. Article and video content builds trust in your expertise. Retarget motivated sellers across devices and platforms. Provide 24/7 accessibility via chatbots. The online world is your marketplace.

Leverage technology to uncover opportunities. Automated valuation models efficiently filter for underpriced properties and distressed motivated sellers. Lead generation sites deliver real-time prospects. Data mining identifies inheritance sellers and other niche scenarios. Tech provides a steady pipeline.

Evaluate emerging models like iBuyers with an open mind. Some sellers prioritize convenience over maximized profit. Blend aspects of the iBuyer functionality they find appealing into your offerings. Meet sellers' needs on their terms, not yours.

Embrace innovation, but keep the human element. While technology opens new doors, people crave trusted advisors when making major financial decisions. Share your experience navigating previous housing cycles. Be transparent about your own investment strategies and portfolio. Authenticity builds connections algorithms can't match.

Stay educated on the latest real estate tech trends. Attend industry conferences and read tech-focused media. Pilot promising new CRM, contract management or online advertising tools. Visit model homes flaunting cutting-edge smart home automation. Don't get complacent playing catch up. Stay on the leading edge.

The real estate landscape will continue rapidly evolving. Investors focused on delivering value by fusing high-tech capabilities with personal expertise will own the future. Let technology accelerate and enhance how you solve problems, not replace the relationships and insight that ultimately drive success.

Key Takeaways Across Market Conditions

Real estate investors must remain vigilant students across market cycles. Don't rely on stale playbooks when contexts change. Consistently hone your ability to read data, build networks and creatively serve motivated sellers.

In sellers' markets, set yourself apart by uncovering hidden opportunities and removing obstacles to get deals done when inventory is scarce. During buyers' booms, position yourself as a trusted navigator by providing solutions to sellers confused by the abundance of options.

When markets whipsaw, draw stability from adaptable operations and deep relationships to smoothly ride fluctuating waves. Keep integrating the latest real estate technology innovations, while retaining the human touch.

The mark of a great investor isn't flawless execution in calm times, but resilience and innovation through volatility. Motivated sellers partner with experts who consistently identify and deliver opportunities tailored to the moment.

Market dynamics will continuously evolve beyond your control. But by committing to lifelong mastery of the data, tools and connections that enable understanding and adaptation, you build a foundational agility at the core of repeated success across every type of real estate cycle. Your reliable guidance attracts motivated sellers regardless of conditions.

Stay curious, creative and compassionate. With authentic desire to help motivated sellers navigate uncertainty and achieve financial goals, your leadership will be sought when markets swing. Keep learning, innovating and growing through challenge and change. The opportunities to build your real estate empire await across every turn of the market.

CHAPTER 4

Networking and Relationship Building

"It's not what you know, it's who you know." - Anonymous

Build Your Real Estate Empire Through Relationships

Networking is the Lifeblood of Success

Deals happen through trusted connections. **Surround yourself with the right people.**

- Attend industry events. Share, learn and find partners.
- Join mastermind groups. Brainstorm and grow through peer exchanges.
- Build local networks. Know contractors, attorneys, agents in your region.
- Go beyond transactions. Cultivate genuine, lasting relationships.

Be Generous and Engaged

Success is collective. Give value to get value.

- Share insights and advice. Offer your expertise to help others grow.
- Make warm introductions. Connect people who can collaborate.
- Follow up and follow through. Be known as reliable and responsive.
- Don't just take. Find ways to provide meaningful contributions.

Forge Tight Bonds with Agents

Partnerships with agents unlock hidden deals. Earn their trust.

- Close deals quickly. Demonstrate you're serious and deliver results.
- Be ultra professional. Respect their time and needs.
- Offer win-win terms. Structure deals so everyone succeeds.
- Communicate proactively. Update agents frequently so they know they can depend on you.

Build a Standout Online Presence

- Showcase expertise on LinkedIn. Share advice and build authority.
- Engage on industry forums. Ask and answer questions to give back.
- Create valuable content. Educate and attract potential partners.
- Be consistent. Stay top of mind through ongoing participation.

Real estate is a people business. Surround yourself with motivated, trustworthy players who bring out your best. The right relationships unlock exponential success.

Why Networking is Vital for Real Estate Investors

The most prolific real estate investors recognize that deals and opportunities flow through trusted relationships. While novice investors often fixate on lead generation tactics and lower-level hustling, building a robust and generous network pays exponentially greater dividends over time.

Savvy investors immerse themselves in their local real estate community by attending meetups, conferences, and continuing education events. These provide invaluable connections to like-minded investors, agents, lenders and other professionals essential to success.

By regularly participating in mastermind groups, investors can brainstorm deals, benefit from collective insights on market conditions, and forge accountable partnerships to achieve growth goals. Close peer groups illuminate blind spots and provide much-needed support during inevitable downs in the market.

Regional connections in your geographic area are equally important. Knowing local hard money lenders, contractors, estate attorneys and inspectors provides critical resources you can depend on. These relationships also feed you off-market deals before they are broadly advertised. Maintain strong connections in your territory.

While most novice investors focus narrowly on immediate deal objectives, successful players build genuine relationships that span decades. They collaborative freely with their network without expecting immediate reciprocation. Strong connections outlast individual transactions.

By giving value freely through mentorship, knowledge sharing and meaningful introductions, you gain a reputation as a connector who lifts up the entire community. You reap those seeds exponentially when your network rallies around you during challenging periods.

Maximizing Partnerships with Real Estate Agents

Agents are conduits to incredible deal flow if you cultivate win-win partnerships built on trust and transparency. Earn their respect by quickly closing transactions and avoiding time-wasting false starts.

Honor agents' time by being ultra professional. Promptly provide requested paperwork and updates to keep deals moving forward seamlessly. Make yourself an investor agents want to work with.

Offer fair terms that enable agents to prosper while also achieving your return goals. Avoid extreme lowball offers that waste everyone's efforts on unrealistic expectations. Find the win-win.

Communicate early and often so agents feel informed. Give frequent progress updates and involve them in problem solving. Respond quickly to inquiries. The more agents trust you, the more opportunities come your way.

Patience and playing the long game pays off with agents. One bad experience can unravel multiple future deals. Consistently build positive experiences together.

By being a reliable, honest and reasonable partner, you become the investor agents think of first when an off-market opportunity arises. You gain access to inventory that never hits the challenging open market.

Build an Influential Online Presence

In addition to in-person networking, establishing your expertise and personal brand online opens new doors through expanded reach. An active, professional digital presence attracts potential partners globally.

LinkedIn is a must. Share advice and perspectives through posts and articles. Comment on others' content to engage in constructive discussions. Building authority expands your influence and network.

Participate on industry forums and in Facebook groups to exchange ideas with fellow investors. Ask smart questions and provide thoughtful answers to build credibility. Become a valuable member of each community.

Create free educational content like how-to guides, neighborhood analyses, and market trend reports. This demonstrates your passion for adding value beyond promoting yourself. Useful content builds lasting mindshare.

Post consistently across networks and platforms. Stay top of mind so fellow investors are comfortable reaching out for deals, partnerships and insights. Ongoing participation compounds relationships over time.

While in-person relationships will always be essential, your digital network magnifies opportunities. Blend old-school networking values of generosity and service with new-school digital tools.

The most successful real estate investors continuously expand their network's reach and depth. They embrace opportunities to learn from others while also sharing hard-won wisdom. Relationships are the lifeblood; cultivate them intentionally.

Key Takeaways on Networking

- Real estate is a team sport. Surround yourself with others who are hungry, ethical and ambitious.
- Give value freely without expecting instant reciprocity. Generosity and engagement build goodwill over years.
- Nurture win-win partnerships with agents. Deliver reliability, transparency and professionalism.
- Establish influence online through consistent content and engagement. Become a recognized voice.
- Stay active. Attend events, facilitate introductions and provide support. Invest time in relationships.

The foundation of sustainable success is a robust network of trusted advisors, partners and collaborators. Skilled investors understand this secret. They know fruitful deals and exponential growth flow through meaningful connections.

Don't buy into the myth of the lone wolf investor. Take a collaborative, community-focused approach based on mutual benefit. Give to receive. Offer wisdom to gain wisdom.

The relationships and reputation you cultivate will pay dividends for the rest of your investing career. Keep your network nourished and expanding. Abundant deals, resources and fulfillment will naturally spring forth.

CHAPTER 5

The Importance of Research

"The more you know about the past, the better prepared you are for the future." - Theodore Roosevelt

The Path to Real Estate Riches: Master the Art of Research

Legendary investors understand a fundamental truth: Comprehensive research and insights separate the pros from the amateurs. Informed decisions unlock exponential returns while guesswork invites catastrophe. Treat lifelong learning as your superpower.

Become a Relentless Student of Your Markets

Thriving investors obsess over accumulating granular knowledge about their territory. They immerse themselves in data, news and training to spot opportunities faster than anyone.

Analyze Reams of Historical Data

Study sales trends and pricing at the neighborhood and block level going back decades. Understand seasonality patterns and market cycles. Identify leading indicators that signal shifts early. Granular data reveals hidden gems.

Track Supply and Demand Dynamics

Monitor which neighborhoods see inventory sell rapidly versus languish. High-demand, low-supply areas offer ripe opportunities. Watch for new construction and remodels expanding inventory. Know where competitors are crowding in.

Follow Local Developments Closely

Drive target neighborhoods frequently, watching for new projects breaking ground. Permit applications and regulatory changes telegraph future shifts. Subscribe to town planning emails and attend meetings. Insider info provides a competitive edge.

Go Micro with Perspective

Details matter. One side of a street can be far more valuable than the other based on amenities like parks. No amount of research is too small. Micro insights yield mega results.

Never Stop Expanding Your Knowledge

Voracious learning separates the pros from the pretenders. Read industry media daily to stay fluent in innovation and linguo. Take regular training classes on financial modeling, negotiations, rehabbing advances. Join peer mastermind groups to exchange intel. Information fuels success.

Uncover Hidden Motivated Seller Gems

Motivated sellers rarely advertise their circumstances publicly. You must proactively excavate opportunities before competitors.

Mine Public Records for Nuggets

Monitor new divorce filings, deaths, code violations, lawsuits, property tax delinquencies, etc. Life events lead to distress sales below market value. Public records provide a treasure trove of potential off-market deals.

Harness Online Sources

Websites list upcoming foreclosure auctions, loan defaults, probate sales and other time-sensitive deals. Distressed sellers will often accept lowball offers to quickly exit disadvantageous positions.

Leverage Your Local Network

Ask your connections for rumors of owners planning to sell before officially listing. Well-connected players catch wind of deals first. Build relationships with agents and contractors who tend to hear of opportunities.

Have Authentic Conversations

Attend local events and engage residents in genuine dialogue. If they trust your intent, people will open up about their situations and challenges. In-person interactions build fertile ground for deals.

Pick the Brains of Industry Veterans

Buy tacos and pick the brains of commercial real estate lawyers, brokers, developers, contractors, etc. with decades of experience. Their accumulated knowledge about the market's history and players is invaluable.

Do Your Diligence Before Committing

Once potential deals arise, meticulous due diligence protects you from making overpriced offers or sinking money into duds. Leave no stone unturned.

Crunch All the Numbers

Verify the accuracy of seller claims about repairs required. Hire experienced inspectors to identify issues. Vet comparables thoroughly. Calculate ROI conservatively to build in margin for error. Question every assumption.

Master the Fine Print

Study property history, permits, zoning, rent control rules, noise ordinances, existing liens and every other minute detail. Talk with regulators to understand constraints and options. Don't take anything at face value.

Build an All-Star Team

Rely on specialists like real estate attorneys, CPAs, architects, engineers, designers, etc. Their insights will prove invaluable. Don't let ego lead you to go it alone. Leverage experts' experience.

Model Multiple Scenarios

Create detailed pro formas projecting costs, timelines and exit strategies under best/worst case assumptions. Stress test opportunities from every angle. Ensure adequate reserves and contingency plans if issues arise. Think through every branch in decision trees.

Solicit Peer Review

Before committing large amounts of capital, run deals by trusted fellow investors to identify potential flaws in your reasoning. Do the numbers seem aggressive or conservative? What am I missing? Avoid confirmation bias by actively seeking criticism.

Commit to Lifelong Learning

Real estate investing is a dynamic field requiring constant education. Falling behind on industry evolution leads to missed opportunities and costly mistakes.

Stay Immersed in Media

Read industry publications daily. Follow influential blogs, podcasts and video channels. Absorb important statistics, evolving business models, technological advances, financing innovations, etc. Fluency with info provides a competitive edge.

Take Regular Training Classes

Never stop acquiring new skills. Take courses on negotiation tactics, creative real estate financing, advanced rehabbing techniques, blockchain applications - whatever expands your capabilities. Stagnation means death in this business.

Observe Top Performers

Study peers who consistently drive exceptional results. What are they doing differently in deal sourcing, development, marketing or management? Model the behaviors of those achieving the returns you seek.

Question Assumptions

The conventional "rules" are often outdated. Scrutinize established industry practices from first principles. How could new technologies or business models upend current real estate norms? Stale assumptions create blind spots.

Join Masterminds

Brainstorm challenges and opportunities with peer groups experiencing similar issues at higher levels. Mastermind members serve as invaluable sounding boards providing win-win accountability and support. I suggest looking into the Investor Harvest Mastermind at https://Investorharvest.com.

Conclusion

The divide between mediocrity and mastery in real estate comes down to knowledge. Agents fixated on hasty deals spin wheels in frustration. Informed investors spot opportunities early and prosper mightily.

Treat research and learning with an abundance mindset. More data, more informed decisions, more success. Scale up expertise over decades through compound knowledge.

The lure of real estate riches attracts an endless swarm of underprepared newbies. But fortunes flow to those humble and diligent enough to master the craft. Put in your 10,000 hours. Learn, refine, experiment, adapt and actualize mastery.

Success comes to those who hedge risks through diligence and see around corners through wisdom. Knowledge enables you to play chess when others play checkers. Embrace your inner nerd and flourish.

The call is clear: Outwork, outresearch, outstrategize. Stay addicted to information gain. Let obsessive learning propel you to the peaks of real estate achievement. Champions are forged through eternal education. Your time is now.

CHAPTER 6

Effective Lead Generation Techniques

"Success in real estate is not just about finding leads; it's about mastering the art of effective lead generation." - Shawn Tiberio

The Art of Magnetizing Motivated Seller Leads

Thriving real estate investors recognize that consistently generating a high volume of quality motivated seller leads is the lifeblood of their business. They dedicate themselves to mastering multiple lead generation strategies, testing relentlessly, and optimizing based on data. For them, attracting ideal prospects is a science and an art form.

Perfecting the Art of Direct Mail

In an increasingly digital world, effective direct mail campaigns can capture attention and spark meaningful connections with potential sellers unlike anything else. But simply spraying mailers en masse is fruitless. Thoughtfully crafted, personalized and tested direct mail dominates.

Get Personal With Customization

Personalize every aspect including handwritten envelope addresses, customized letters mentioning recipients' home values, and incentives tailored to their likely motivations. This level of personalization makes your mailers feel like 1:1 communication instead of bulk pitches.

Speak to Their Hopes, Fears and Motivations

Understand your ideal customer segments intimately. Know the problems that keep them up at night and craft messages specifically addressing how you can solve those pains. The more your mailers demonstrate genuine empathy for recipients' situations the more they will resonate.

Vividly Paint a Picture of Success

Use descriptive language and visuals to showcase how working with you will alleviate stress and open new doors. Help them imagine the relief they'll feel or exciting opportunities ahead if they partner with you. Vivid success stories are persuasive. Don't just state benefits; bring them to life.

Sprinkle Urgency and Scarcity

Limited-time offers, exclusive access and other urgent calls-to-action can incentivize contacting you. But use scarcity strategically vs sounding desperate. You want to convey special opportunity without pressuring. Find the right balance.

Continuously Test and Optimize

Regularly refresh your designs, offers and target segments. Monitor response rates and conversion closely. Experiment with time of day, list sources, subject lines and other variables to refine your approach. Even slight optimizations add up. Never get complacent with direct mail.

Mastering Digital Marketing

Your website and online presence are like 24/7 digital magnets attracting ideal prospects. They must instantly build credibility and make it easy for visitors to engage further. Optimization is key to converting strangers into leads.

Build SEO Authority with Quality Content

Create articles, FAQs, neighborhood guides and other content optimized for keywords buyers search. Valuable information earns organic rankings and traffic. Target informational queries vs transactional ones (e.g. "how to sell inherited home" vs. "home buyers in Dallas").

Launch Targeted PPC Campaigns

Use pay-per-click ads to amplify reach, targeting motivated sellers based on factors like geography, demographics, income and home value. Send traffic to landing pages tailored to each ad theme for higher conversion. Test various audience segments and messaging.

Engage on Social Media

Focus less on promoting yourself and more on building community by sharing useful perspectives. Respond to every comment. Humanize your expertise so you become a trusted resource vs salesperson.

Retarget Engaged Visitors

Use ads to re-engage website visitors after they've left to keep you top of mind, nudging them to convert over time. Remarketing helps you cost-effectively stay in front of warm leads.

Obsess Over Conversion Tracking

Monitor website analytics religiously to understand how visitors flow through your site and where they drop off. Kill underperforming campaigns, double down on what works and continuously optimize for conversions.

Becoming a Content Machine

Valuable educational content establishes you as an authority buyers can trust. You magnetize leads by generously giving practical, engaging info. Consistency and quality rule.

Address the Questions Buyers Have

Create content that provides helpful solutions to challenges your targets face. Optimize blogs and videos for informational queries. If you rank well organically, buyers will find you when seeking answers.

Vary Content Types and Topics

Mix up blogs, videos, guides, quizzes, webinars and Q&As focused on diverse issues motivated sellers care about. Offer a wealth of media tailored to different learning styles. Fresh content keeps buyers engaged.

Repurpose Content Across Channels

Take a blog post and rehash it as a social media post, email newsletter blurb, infographic and video script. Maximize content mileage by distributing it everywhere.

Analyze Performance Meticulously

Monitor traffic and engagement metrics for each piece of content. Double down on topics and formats that resonate most. Let data inform your content strategy and calendar.

Collaborate with Industry Peers

Reach out to other real estate investors you respect and co-create content. Cross-promote each other. Combining perspectives brings well-rounded insights buyers crave.

Turn Contacts into Advocates

Nothing generates high-quality leads like referrals from existing satisfied clients and partners. You must nurture relationships to earn this loyalty.

Share Your Expertise Freely

Don't look at other investors as competitors. Position yourself as a resource to associations, agents, lenders etc. by providing insights that make them look good to clients.

Stay Top of Mind

Check in regularly with your network to give updates, share interesting ideas and ask thoughtful questions. Add value without always selling.

Go Above and Beyond to Help Partners Succeed

When fellow investors or agents you work with score wins, find ways to celebrate their success and get involved in promoting them. A rising tide lifts all boats.

Express Sincere Gratitude

Thank every referral source through thoughtful gestures and appreciative communication. People love recognition. Find meaningful ways to convey your gratitude.

Request Referrals Smoothly

When appropriate, use soft closes like "I appreciate connecting, please keep me in mind if you or someone you know could use my services." Make it easy for contacts to refer you.

Becoming an Education Destination

Hosting seminars establishes you as an approachable expert while nurturing leads. Make events engaging vs dry lectures.

Solve Key Problems on Attendees' Minds

Survey past clients and prospects on their most pressing questions when considering selling. Design sessions around addressing those concerns through teaching and group discussion.

Encourage Audience Participation

Get attendees involved through polls, Q&As and small group breakouts. This interaction results in higher trust and recall than one-way lectures.

Record and Repurpose Content

Reshare workshop recordings and highlights in your newsletter, on social media and as standalone online videos to benefit those who couldn't attend live. Expand reach.

Follow Up to Continue Nurturing

Send personalized emails recapping key takeaways. Share additional resources that build on concepts discussed. Transition them into your ongoing lead nurturing system.

Offer Incentives for Registration

Give discounts, access to exclusive content libraries or entry into giveaways to incentivize signups. Free events still require registration so you capture lead info.

Partner Up with Real Estate Wholesalers

Alliances with investors who specialize in off-market deal sourcing provide leveraged access to inventory not publicly listed yet. But incentives must be aligned.

Create Win-Win Affiliate Programs

Formalize referral partnerships where wholesalers earn a % of profits from leads that close successful deals. This incentivizes proactive deal flow their way.

Co-Host Events to Widen Reach

Pool resources and invite lists to host larger seminars, networking meetups and workshops together. More motivated sellers to interact with in one place.

Exchange Market Intel

Regularly share emerging opportunities, neighborhoods with supply/demand shifts, and updates on your target buyer profiles. A larger shared knowledge base benefits everyone.

Ensure Mutual Success

They should earn only when you close profitable deals from their leads. Payment upon closing motivates the wholesaler to bring high-quality opportunities.

Integrate CRMs

Use connected agent/investor customer relationship management tools to seamlessly track deal flow between you. Shared systems facilitate collaboration.

Launch Targeted Lead Capture Sites

Dedicated "microsites" focused on specific niches, locations and motivated seller needs help attract and capture relevant prospects. But compelling offers are crucial.

Customize Messaging and Images

Tailor copy, photos, neighborhood references and testimonials to closely reflect each target niche. If the site seems generic, response rates will be poor.

Gate Valuable Resources Visitors Want

Offer free market reports, neighborhood-specific guides, property valuation tools, savings calculators etc. in exchange for contact info through lead forms.

Promptly Nurture New Leads

Provide series of value-packed follow-up emails. Send interesting local insights, event invites and personalized offers. Build a relationship beyond the initial hook.

Test a Variety of Appeals

Experiment with different headlines, graphic styles, lead magnet offers, and calls to action. Track conversions to optimize effectiveness.

Obsess Over Data and Testing

Sophisticated real estate investors know generating quality leads isn't luck. It results from continuously testing, measuring and optimizing their marketing machine.

Track Every Conversion and Engagement Metric

Monitor website analytics, ad platform data, email open/click rates, landing page conversion rates, cost per lead and everything in between. Measure relentlessly.

Run Rigorous A/B Experiments

Regularly test email subject lines, copy, landing page designs, calls to action, lead magnet offers etc. against each other. Let the data guide optimization.

Mine Your CRM for Insights

Analyze why some prospects convert to clients quickly vs slowly or never at all. Look for patterns around lead source, demographic data and engagement metrics you can leverage.

Automate Tracking and Reporting

Use tools like Google Analytics, Facebook Pixel, LinkedIn Insights etc. to automatically pull key metrics instead of manual analysis. Focus on strategy over routine reporting.

The best marketers are eternal students. They continuously hone their expertise at attracting ideal prospects through refinement and innovation. Lead generation mastery compounds over years. But the effort pays exponential dividends.

CHAPTER 7

Mastering Communication

"Communication works for those who work at it." - John Powell

Effective communication is a cornerstone of success in the real estate industry. As the seventh silent killer that could hinder your real estate business's growth, poor communication can lead to misunderstandings, missed opportunities, and failed deals. In this chapter, we'll explore the art of mastering communication with potentially motivated sellers, fellow professionals, and other stakeholders in the real estate process.

1. Empathy and Active Listening:

Approaching every interaction with empathy and genuine interest in the needs and concerns of motivated sellers is a fundamental principle that underpins effective communication in the realm of real estate. This approach signifies a commitment to understanding the unique circumstances that sellers may be navigating. By immersing yourself in their perspectives and demonstrating a heartfelt curiosity about their objectives, you establish a strong foundation for meaningful dialogue.

The skill of active listening stands as a powerful tool within your repertoire. Through active listening, you transcend mere exchange of words and delve into the nuances that define sellers' motivations and preferences. This intentional practice enables you to decode the subtle cues that might shape their decisions, thereby providing you with a more comprehensive understanding of their outlook.

However, the true essence of establishing rapport goes beyond just listening; it encompasses acknowledging sellers' emotions and actively engaging with their narratives. This dynamic approach fosters an atmosphere of mutual respect and understanding. By validating their feelings and demonstrating your investment in their stories, you establish a bridge of trust that spans the gap between transactional interaction and genuine connection.

In the broader context of negotiations, this approach serves as a solid stepping stone. By cultivating trust and rapport, you pave the way for more productive conversations. Sellers are more likely to engage openly with someone who values their concerns and takes the time to understand their needs. This foundation of trust encourages open and transparent discussions, ultimately leading to more favorable outcomes for all parties involved.

In summation, approaching interactions with empathy, active listening, and a willingness to engage on an emotional level creates a powerful framework for establishing rapport. This rapport serves as a bedrock for successful negotiations and lays the groundwork for long-lasting relationships. As you consistently apply these principles, you enhance your ability to navigate the complexities of the real estate landscape with finesse and achieve mutually beneficial results.

2. Clarity and Transparency:

Effective and transparent communication plays a pivotal role in the intricate web of real estate transactions. The clarity of your messages is of paramount importance, requiring a deliberate effort to steer clear of convoluted jargon or perplexing language. Embracing straightforwardness, you impart information with precision, leaving no room for misinterpretation or uncertainty.

Within this realm of clear communication, it is imperative to expound upon the process, the intricacies of terms, and the nuanced conditions that shape the transaction. By meticulously detailing these aspects, you create a tapestry of understanding that leaves no gaps or shadows for ambiguity to reside. This meticulousness cultivates an environment where motivated sellers can navigate the landscape with assurance, knowing that their questions and concerns are comprehensively addressed.

Transparency, in its essence, stands as the cornerstone of this communication approach. It is through this transparency that you forge a connection of confidence and assurance. Sellers, when met with an open and forthcoming attitude, are more likely to feel at ease, trusting that their interests are genuinely valued and protected.

Ultimately, the significance of clear and transparent communication extends beyond mere transactions. It signifies the cultivation of relationships built on honesty, respect, and mutual understanding. As you consistently uphold these principles in your communication, you create a legacy of professionalism and trustworthiness in the realm of real estate.

3. Effective Negotiation:

Effective negotiation is a pivotal element within the landscape of real estate transactions. The refinement of negotiation skills can significantly influence the trajectory of outcomes, shaping the path toward successful agreements. A nuanced blend of strategy and finesse defines this art, where the aim is to craft solutions that bridge the divide between motivated sellers' aspirations and your investment objectives.

In this orchestration of negotiation, the spotlight falls upon the art of reaching resolutions that satisfy all parties involved. The focus extends beyond transactional endpoints, delving into the heart of collaborative understanding. This perspective gives rise to the pursuit of win-win scenarios, where the needs of motivated sellers harmoniously interweave with the cadence of your investment goals.

This journey requires a patient navigation through the intricate twists and turns of discussions. Patience becomes the cornerstone, offering a steady foundation upon which agreements can be built organically. Flexibility, too, emerges as a key ingredient, enabling you to explore the terrain of alternatives and adaptations that can cater to diverse needs.

Enter the realm of creativity, a sphere that encourages the exploration of uncharted avenues. Here, ingenuity is your ally, allowing you to devise solutions that may lie beyond conventional boundaries. This spirit of innovation introduces novel perspectives, enriching the negotiation process and broadening the spectrum of possibilities.

Negotiation serves as the nucleus of real estate dynamics, where strategic calculation coalesces with intuitive judgment, and the art of compromise converges with structured discourse. Remember, it's not solely about finalizing transactions; it's about fostering connections, shaping outcomes that echo with integrity and foresight. As you navigate this territory, you hold the reins of influence, sculpting agreements that stand as testaments to effective negotiation skills.

4. Timeliness and Responsiveness:

In the dynamic world of real estate, the cadence of time holds profound significance. Swift and timely responses to inquiries and interactions with motivated sellers are akin to the rhythmic beats that propel the melody of successful transactions. The importance of this tempo cannot be understated, for in its absence, the harmony of opportunity might wane, allowing alternate chords to take center stage.

Embracing timeliness, however, extends beyond mere speed. It's a statement of dedication, a testament to your professionalism in an environment where swift adaptation is a hallmark of success. By punctuating your communication with a rhythm that matches the tempo of the industry, you infuse your interactions with a sense of urgency that aligns with the fast-moving currents of real estate.

Furthermore, this rhythm is a bridge to credibility. Sellers, driven by their own timelines and aspirations, appreciate responsiveness as a sign of respect. It reflects your recognition of their needs and acknowledges the value of their time. As you orchestrate your responses, each note resonates with the essence of professionalism, creating a harmonious composition that bolsters your reputation in the eyes of motivated sellers.

Remember, in this symphony of real estate, the staccato of timeliness can uplift your performance, forging connections that reverberate with trust and authenticity. Each response is a note in the score of opportunity, and your skillful navigation of this tempo can render a masterpiece of engagement that crescendos toward success.

5. Professionalism in Written Communication:

Effective written communication is a cornerstone of professionalism in the world of real estate. It serves as a clear reflection of your reliability and credibility, shaping the way you interact with motivated sellers and other stakeholders. Written communication takes various forms, such as emails and messages, and plays a pivotal role in conveying agreements, proposals, and crucial information accurately.

In the landscape of real estate transactions, proper grammar and formal language are akin to the notes that create harmony. Just as a composer carefully selects each note, you must choose your words thoughtfully to ensure that your messages resonate with precision and clarity. The way you structure your sentences and convey your thoughts reflects your attention to detail and your commitment to professionalism.

Moreover, written communication is more than just words on a page; it's the blueprint for understanding and collaboration. Like an architect designing a building, you meticulously craft your messages to ensure that agreements are outlined clearly, leaving no room for ambiguity. Your written words become the foundation upon which trust is built, creating a framework of reliability and transparency.

Each written interaction is an opportunity to showcase your professionalism. Whether it's a formal email outlining terms or a casual message discussing next steps, your communication style reflects your dedication to excellence. Just as a masterpiece is composed stroke by stroke, your messages contribute to the larger narrative of your reputation as a trusted and dependable professional.

In the dynamic field of real estate, written communication serves as the bridge that connects you with motivated sellers and fellow industry members. By adhering to the principles of clarity, proper grammar, and professionalism, you create a lasting impression that aligns with the values of the industry. Your written words become a testament to your commitment to effective communication and your dedication to fostering positive relationships.

6. Confidence and Poise:

Displaying a sense of confidence and poise is paramount when engaging in the field of real estate. These attributes extend beyond mere self-assurance; they serve as powerful instruments to establish your credibility and authority as a real estate investor. By emanating confidence and maintaining a poised demeanor, you can create a lasting impression that resonates with motivated sellers.

Confidence is a cornerstone that underpins your expertise and knowledge. It's not about flashy displays, but rather a genuine belief in your capabilities and a thorough understanding of the intricacies of the real estate market. When you approach interactions with this unwavering assurance, it sends a clear message to motivated sellers that you are well-versed and capable of navigating the challenges that arise during property transactions.

Poise, in conjunction with confidence, conveys a composed and collected demeanor. It signifies your ability to maintain your equilibrium even in the face of complex negotiations. Poise serves as a reflection of your professionalism, demonstrating that you are prepared to address any questions, concerns, or obstacles that may arise. This sense of self-assuredness adds another layer of trustworthiness to your image.

Together, confidence and poise are potent tools that can sway motivated sellers in your favor. As they witness your assured demeanor, they are more likely to feel at ease in your presence and more willing to engage in meaningful discussions. The aura you project indicates that you are not just an investor seeking transactions but a partner genuinely invested in their best interests.

During conversations, negotiations, and any interaction in the realm of real estate, your confidence and poise are your silent allies. They signify that you are someone who commands respect and can handle negotiations with professionalism and integrity. By portraying these attributes consistently, you create an environment of trust where motivated sellers can confidently enter negotiations, knowing they are dealing with a capable and reliable investor.

As you work to enhance your real estate endeavors, remember that your demeanor speaks volumes. Confidence and poise are not just personal qualities; they are the building blocks of your reputation in the industry. By projecting these attributes in your interactions, you can cultivate relationships based on trust, authority, and credibility. Ultimately, motivated sellers will be drawn to work with someone who radiates confidence and poise, setting the stage for successful transactions and enduring partnerships.

7. Addressing Concerns and Objections:

Motivated sellers often find themselves grappling with uncertainties and objections as they navigate the process of selling their properties. Recognizing these concerns and approaching them with a thoughtful mindset is crucial for establishing a rapport built on understanding and trust. By acknowledging the worries that motivated sellers might have and addressing them in a considerate manner, you can foster an environment where open communication and productive discussions can take place.

When addressing these concerns, it's vital to go beyond mere acknowledgment. Take the time to delve into the core of their worries, seeking to comprehend the underlying reasons for their objections. This depth of understanding allows you to tailor your responses in a way that resonates with their specific situation and motivations. By doing so, you demonstrate your commitment to truly grasping their perspective and working collaboratively to find suitable solutions.

Crafting your responses in a way that aligns your offer with their aspirations and objectives is pivotal. Explain how the terms you propose are designed not only to meet their immediate needs but also to align with their long-term goals. Demonstrating this alignment highlights your intention to create a mutually beneficial outcome, which can significantly enhance their confidence in your proposal.

Furthermore, addressing potential risks transparently is a hallmark of professionalism. Instead of brushing aside concerns, openly discuss any potential pitfalls and outline how you intend to mitigate them. This proactive approach showcases your commitment to a transparent and honest negotiation process. Sellers will appreciate your willingness to tackle challenges head-on, fostering an atmosphere of credibility and trust.

Remember, effective communication is a two-way street. Encourage motivated sellers to share their apprehensions openly and listen attentively to their viewpoints. Your ability to actively engage with their concerns demonstrates your dedication to finding common ground and crafting solutions that work for both parties.

By thoughtfully addressing concerns, objections, and uncertainties, you create an environment of respect and empathy. This environment is conducive to fostering smoother transactions and nurturing relationships built on trust. Your willingness to navigate potential roadblocks with understanding and professionalism can set the stage for successful negotiations and the achievement of shared objectives. Ultimately, the art of addressing concerns transforms potential obstacles into opportunities for collaboration and partnership.

8. Closing the Deal:

In the concluding phases of a real estate transaction, effective communication becomes paramount, particularly in elucidating the intricacies of the closing process and managing expectations. To ensure a seamless and harmonious conclusion, it's imperative to provide sellers with a lucid and comprehensive overview of the necessary steps, critical deadlines, and essential documentation required for a successful closing. By carefully guiding sellers through this critical phase, you can pave the way for an experience that is not only streamlined but also alleviates any potential stress for all parties involved.

At this pivotal juncture, your ability to communicate with precision and clarity plays a pivotal role. Rather than assuming sellers are familiar with the nuances of the closing process, take the initiative to articulate each step in an accessible manner. Provide a step-by-step breakdown of the key milestones, from signing contracts to completing inspections and fulfilling any outstanding contingencies. This detailed outline can serve as a valuable roadmap, helping sellers understand the sequence of events and the anticipated timeline leading up to the closing date.

Furthermore, proactively addressing potential concerns or questions can foster a sense of reassurance. As you outline the process, anticipate common queries that sellers might have and provide thorough explanations. By preemptively addressing uncertainties, you create an atmosphere of transparency and open communication that is essential for a successful closing.

In addition to detailing the procedural aspects, make it clear which documents are required for the closing. Offer guidance on gathering and preparing these documents, highlighting their significance in the transaction. This proactive approach can prevent last-minute scrambling and ensure that the closing process progresses smoothly.

To enhance the experience for all parties, consider offering personalized support tailored to the sellers' specific circumstances. This may include coordinating with legal professionals or providing contacts for reputable service providers who can assist with necessary tasks. By going the extra mile to facilitate a seamless closing, you not only demonstrate your commitment to a successful transaction but also showcase your dedication to delivering exceptional service.

As you guide sellers through the final stages of the real estate transaction, keep lines of communication open and encourage questions. Address any concerns promptly and provide regular updates on the progress of the closing. This level of engagement not only promotes transparency but also fosters a sense of collaboration, reinforcing the shared objective of a successful and timely closing.

In conclusion, the culmination of a real estate transaction hinges on effective communication during the closing process. By presenting a clear and thorough overview of the steps, deadlines, and documentation involved, you empower sellers to navigate this critical phase with confidence. Your guidance not only ensures a seamless and stress-free experience but also underscores your commitment to professionalism and client satisfaction. Through meticulous communication, you pave the way for a closing that is not only successful but also leaves a positive lasting impression.

Conclusion

Becoming a true maestro of communication stands as an indispensable cornerstone of triumph in the dynamic realm of real estate. Through the embodiment of empathy, the art of active listening, the embodiment of clarity, and the exhibition of transparency, you forge resilient connections with motivated sellers that form the bedrock of prosperous partnerships. As you navigate the symphony of negotiation with finesse, punctuality, and unwavering professionalism, you further cement your reputation as a credible and trustworthy player in the industry, fortifying your path toward the fruitful realization of successful deals.

In your pursuit of mastery, address the concerns and objections that might arise with a deft touch. This deft approach not only exhibits your dedication to comprehending the sellers' unique needs but also cultivates a haven of trust and unwavering assurance in your capabilities. The virtuosity you display in managing these intricacies reverberates, resonating with the sellers on a profound level and solidifying your position as a reliable partner in their real estate journey.

It is important to recognize that the orchestration of effective communication isn't a static accomplishment, but an ever-evolving opus. Embrace a spirit of continuous growth, nurturing your skills and honing your techniques to resonate with the changing cadences of the market. As you embark on this journey of refinement, the mastery of communication serves as a potent antidote against the insidious threat of subpar communication.

Ultimately, the culmination of your efforts promises an expanse of opportunities for your real estate enterprise to thrive and flourish. Like an exquisite symphony that captivates the senses, your prowess in communication will harmonize every interaction, foster enduring connections, and unveil avenues that lead to triumphant crescendos of success. So, let the resonant chords of effective communication reverberate throughout your endeavors, dispelling any shadows that might obscure your path, and ushering in a symphony of achievements that echoes for generations to come.

Conclusion

Congratulations on completing "Real Estate Business Funda-mentals!"

In this book, you've explored the seven silent killers that can derail your real estate business before it even gets started:

- Intense competition
- Flawed marketing strategies
- Market conditions and trends
- Networking and relationship building
- The importance of research
- Ineffective lead generation techniques
- Poor communication

By understanding and addressing these challenges, you've gained valuable insights into enhancing your strategies, overcoming obstacles, and propelling your real estate venture toward success.

But your journey doesn't end here. To truly thrive in the real estate industry, you need to embrace the power of continuous learning, adaptability, and perseverance.

Here are a few tips to help you stay ahead of the curve and achieve your real estate goals:

- Embrace innovation and creativity. The real estate industry is constantly evolving, so it's important to stay ahead of the curve by embracing new technologies and innovative marketing strategies.

- Continuously refine your strategies. What worked yesterday may not work tomorrow, so it's crucial to regularly review and refine your approach to ensure you're getting the best possible results.
- Stay informed about the latest market trends and industry developments. The real estate market is constantly fluctuating, so it's important to stay informed about the latest trends and developments to make informed investment decisions.

As you embark on your real estate journey, remember that every challenge presents an opportunity for growth and improvement. Be patient, stay resilient, and leverage the valuable lessons learned in "Real Estate Business Fundamentals" to guide you toward a prosperous future in the world of real estate investing.

Are you ready to take your real estate business to new heights of success? Look no further than REIToolbox!

REIToolbox is the ultimate solution to unlock the full potential of your real estate ventures. Our platform offers a comprehensive suite of cutting-edge tools and resources meticulously crafted to boost your lead generation, streamline marketing efforts, and maximize your investment returns.

With REIToolbox at your side, you can:

- Dominate your local market with a winning marketing strategy tailored to attract motivated sellers.
- Connect with a vibrant community of investors and professionals, opening doors to off-market opportunities.
- Access cutting-edge tools that streamline your lead generation and investment analysis process.

- Leverage the power of data and trends to make informed decisions that yield exceptional returns.

Don't let the silent killers of the real estate industry hold you back any longer. Take action now and join the REIToolbox community—a powerhouse of growth and opportunity.

Get ready to:

- Dominate your local market with a winning marketing strategy tailored to attract motivated sellers.
- Connect with a vibrant community of investors and professionals, opening doors to off-market opportunities.
- Access cutting-edge tools that streamline your lead generation and investment analysis process.
- Leverage the power of data and trends to make informed decisions that yield exceptional returns.

Seize the opportunity to transform your real estate business into an unstoppable force in the market. The time is now to break free from the barriers that hold you back and embark on a journey of boundless growth and success.

Join REIToolbox today and let us be the driving force behind your real estate business's meteoric rise! Take action now and embrace the key to unlocking your real estate dreams with REIToolbox! Book your marketing audit today —> https://reitoolbox.com/leads

Scan Here